W9-ATG-832

ANIMALS AT WORK

Animals
Defending
Themselves

WORLD
BOOK

World Book, Inc.
180 North LaSalle Street
Suite 900
Chicago, Illinois 60601
USA

Produced for World Book, Inc. by Bailey Publishing Associates Ltd.

For information about other World Book publications, visit our website at **www.worldbook.com** or call **1-800-WORLDBK (967-5325)**.

Library of Congress Cataloging-in-Publication data has been applied for.

Title: Animals Defending Themselves
ISBN: 978-0-7166-2728-9

Animals at Work
ISBN: 978-0-7166-2724-1 (set, hc)

Also available as:
ISBN: 978-0-7166-2741-8 (e-book)

Printed in China by Shenzhen Wing King Tong Paper Products Co, Ltd., Shenzhen, Guangdong
1st printing August 2018

4460

Staff

Writer: Sean Connolly

Executive Committee

President
Jim O'Rourke

Vice President and Editor in Chief
Paul A. Kobasa

Vice President, Finance
Donald D. Keller

Vice President, Marketing
Jean Lin

Vice President, International
Maksim Rutenberg

Vice President, Technology
Jason Dole

Director, Human Resources
Bev Ecker

Editorial

Director, Print Publishing
Tom Evans

Managing Editor
Jeff De La Rosa

Editor
William D. Adams

Manager, Contracts & Compliance
(Rights & Permissions)
Loranne K. Shields

Manager, Indexing Services
David Pofelski

Librarian
S. Thomas Richardson

Digital

Director, Digital Product Development
Erika Meller

Digital Product Manager
Jonathan Wills

Manufacturing/Production

Manufacturing Manager
Anne Fritzinger

Proofreader
Nathalie Strassheim

Graphics and Design

Senior Art Director
Tom Evans

Senior Designer
Don Di Sante

Media Editor
Rosalia Bledsoe

Special thanks to:

Roberta Bailey
Nicola Barber
Francis Paola Lea
Claire Munday
Alex Woolf

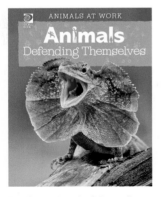

The frilled lizard of Australia unfolds its frill to scare away predators.

Acknowledgments

Cover photo: © Dwi Yulianto, Shutterstock

Alamy: 5 (Photononstop), 6-7 (Dave Watts), 8-9 (Rolf Nussbaumer Photography), 9 (Minden Pictures), 20 (Nature Picture Library), 20-21 (Brian Kushner), 21 (Greatstock), 24 (age footstock), 24-25 (John Sullivan), 30 (john t. fowler), 30-31 (Arterra Picture Library), 33 (kosasp), 39 (Ethan Daniels), 41 (Brandon Cole Marine Photography), 43 (Tom Stack). **Shutterstock**: title page & 12-13 (Victor Lapaev), 4 (Pavlina Basarova), 6 (Hagit Berkovich), 8 (Carol Kelpin), 10 (Rattiya Thongdumhyu), 10-11 (Satit Srihin), 13 (Graeme Shannon), 14-15 (IrinaK), 15 (Daniel Huebner), 17 (Johan Swanepoel), 18-19 (Andrew Sutton), 19 (Beth Swanson), 22-23 (Brendan van Son), 23 (Paula French), 26-27 (Rich Carey), 27 (Roadworks), 28-29 (2630ben), 29 (EcoPrint), 34-35 (Matt Cornish), 35 (Kimree), 36 (Tom Reichner), 36-37 (Tim Gainey), 40-41 (Mr. Meijer), 42 (johannviloria), 42-43 (Matt Jeppson), 44 (James van den Broek), 44-45 (Matt9122).

Contents

Introduction

Many of us are lucky enough to enjoy some security in our everyday lives. We live in safe homes and walk or cycle on safe streets. The job of protecting us often falls to the armed forces, police officers, firefighters, and others.

Animals do not have these protectors. Most of them rely on little more than their instincts—things they know from birth—and their bodies in the daily struggle for survival. Many animals are in constant danger from **predators.** Predators are animals that get their food by killing and eating other animals. To survive, the target of a predator, called **prey,** must defend itself against attack.

The saltwater crocodile is the largest reptile on Earth, and a fearsome predator.

Animal defenses take many forms. Some animals can blend in with their surroundings or find other ways to hide. Others are large and strong enough to fight back and repel a predator. Speed can be used for defense, enabling an animal to outrun, outfly, or outswim a chasing predator.

In this book, you will read about some of the many ways prey animals try to avoid being eaten. Sometimes these methods fail—if they were always successful, all predators would starve to death. But these defensive methods do improve the prey animals' chance of survival.

A natural cycle

Interactions between predator and prey are a major driver of natural selection. *Natural selection* is a process in nature by which the living things best suited to their environment are more likely to survive and reproduce, passing good traits to their offspring. For example, if a predator chases its prey, it is more likely to catch and kill slower individuals. Faster individuals are more likely to survive and reproduce, passing on speedy traits to their offspring. Over time, the prey **species** may become faster overall. Natural selection will favor faster predators in the same way.

A group
of small fish
swims away from
an attacking
shark.

Hiding

The most basic defense against **predators** is simply not to be found. Some **prey** animals live in, or escape to, hard-to-find hiding places. Others blend in with their surroundings or only move about when predators are not around.

BLENDING IN

One of the most familiar ways animals defend themselves is **camouflage.** Just as soldiers may wear clothing to match desert or jungle landscapes, animals can blend in to avoid being seen. Different **species** can camouflage themselves against many natural backdrops, including rain forests, snowfields, and even the kelp and coral of the ocean floor.

The leaf katydid, a relative of crickets and grasshoppers, has broad green wings that look like leaves. This appearance is an excellent defense against such predators as birds, bats, and spiders. Stick **insects** look like twigs. They are almost impossible to see among the branches of trees or bushes where they live.

The leaf katydid has the same color and markings as the leaf it sits on.

The tawny frogmouth, an owl-like bird of Australia, uses excellent camouflage to rest in trees during the day without being seen. Only the bird's bright reddish-orange eyes can give it away. The frogmouth keeps its eyes wide open at night, when there is less need to hide from such predators as eagles. But during the day, the tawny frogmouth narrows its eyelids to tiny slits, so it can peek out at its surroundings without blowing its cover.

A tawny frogmouth and its chick (left) rely on camouflage to stay safe during the day.

Hiding saves energy

Running from a predator or fighting back takes lots of energy. Hiding, by contrast, helps the prey animal conserve, or save, energy. Hiding can leave the prey with more energy for other tasks, such as finding its own food.

CHANGING COLOR

Many animals can blend in with one background. But some have the ability to blend into several different backgrounds. For example, many animals change their coloration with the seasons, particularly in colder areas. Brown fur or feathers—ideal **camouflage** against a wooded background in summer—give way to white coloration as winter snows arrive. The ptarmigan (*TAHR muh guhn*) is a bird that lives in cold northern areas. For half the year, its white coat helps it blend in with the ice and snow. During the brief warm season, the bird molts (sheds) its white feathers, replacing them with a brown coat.

In the winter months, the ptarmigan's white feathers help it blend in with its snowy surroundings.

Rather than changing with the seasons, a few animals can change how they look in minutes or seconds. The bat-faced toad blends in with the colorful scattered leaves and twigs on the floor of South America's tropical forests. It can change its coloring to match a particular pattern of shapes and colors. Many flatfish use the same method to blend in against sand, mud, or pebbles on the ocean floor.

Many **cephalopods** can dramatically change their color in the blink of an eye. Their skin is covered with cells called **chromatophores,** which contain tiny pouches of different-colored **pigment.** Cephalopods squeeze or relax muscles near these cells to change their skin color instantly. Some also have patches of skin called papillae (*puh PIHL ee)* that can be raised into bumps or other shapes. The papillae serve to break up the animal's outline, making it even harder to see. A cephalopod uses its large eyes and brain to take in its surroundings and figure out how best to hide itself.

Disguise for attack and defense

The Merlet's scorpionfish lives in the shallow tropical waters of the Indian and Pacific oceans. There, it hides among coral and sponges, with its bright red, yellow, and black mouth tentacles and skin flaps swaying in the water. Scientists think that the camouflage serves two purposes. First, the mazelike pattern of flaps and tentacles, so much like the surrounding sea floor, lures smaller fish in to be quickly swallowed. Second, the bright colors also may warn away **predators**—the scorpionfish can unleash powerful **venom** from its spines.

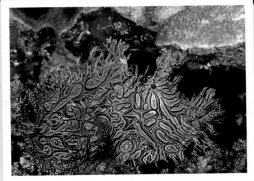

The coloring and mazelike patterns of the Merlet's scorpionfish are excellent camouflage on the sea floor.

Spot the bat-faced toad, well-hidden in the leaf litter of the forest floor in the Amazon rain forest.

NIGHTTIME BEHAVIOR

Animals can avoid **predators** by being active at times when predators are less likely to be around. Most animals do so by moving about night, when many predators are less active. This adaptation is called **nocturnality.** Fruit bats **roost** in daylight high up in trees, where they are safer from snakes and weasels. They wait until night to go out on their long food-gathering flights. The darkness protects them from such predators as snakes and hawks. Wood mice have bulging eyes and large ears to help them find their way around at night, giving them a defensive advantage against foxes, weasels, and house cats.

AVOIDANCE BEHAVIOR

Perhaps the simplest way to avoid being eaten is simply to stay out of a predator's way. All animals that move do this to some extent. Zebras, for example, will not go near an area where they know lions could be found.

Some animals have taken this avoidance behavior to literally another level. The largest migration of living creatures is not the seasonal journey taken by many birds, fish, or **insects.** It involves much smaller living things, called **zooplankton** (*ZOH uh plangk tuhn),* and it takes place each day in the oceans. Zooplankton eat tiny living things called **algae.** Algae, like plants, need light to make food, so they live near the ocean's surface. Zooplankton spend their daylight hours in deeper waters, hiding from such predators as fish and whales. When darkness falls, the zooplankton come to the surface to eat algae. Scientists estimate that this daily migration involves a total weight of more than 21 billion tons (19 billion metric tons) of zooplankton worldwide.

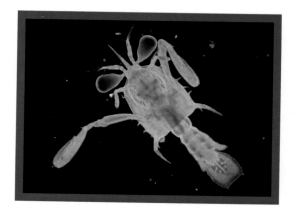

A crab larva, seen through a microscope, is an example of zooplankton.

Giant fruit bats wrap their wings around their bodies to conserve heat as they roost high up in trees during the day.

Escape

If a **predator** has spotted a **prey** animal and starts closing in, the prey may have only one option: escape. Making a successful getaway depends on many factors. An effective escape path must take into account the landscape, the weather, and the skills and habits of the particular predator.

USING SPEED

In some **habitats,** animals can hide easily until the threat of a predator passes. But many more habitats are exposed. Hiding may be impossible in such settings as broad plains, flat deserts, open oceans, and the sky. The only way to get away from a pursuer is to be quicker, or to find a way to turn a predator's speed against it.

The ability to escape quickly is important on the East African **savanna.** There, herds of hoofed animals feed on the grassy plains, which are patrolled by such speedy predators as leopards and cheetahs. Slender antelope are built for speed and often outrun chasing predators. Even stockier grazing animals can speed up quickly and keep up high speeds in escape. Wildebeests, for example, can cruise at up to 50 miles (80 kilometers) per hour.

Some animals must use speed to get away from others of the same **species.** Baby sharks are born knowing how to swim— partly to hunt, but also to escape from adult sharks. Other fish, such as mackerel and bluefish, make use of their streamlined shape to move quickly, whether they are hunting or being hunted.

A cheetah usually hunts its prey in the cooler parts of the day— early morning or just before sunset.

Speedy snake

Predators sometimes need to escape from other predators. Africa's black mamba is one of the world's deadliest snake because of its powerful **venom.** It is also one of the fastest moving snakes in the world. But even this killer has to watch out for predators, usually those striking from above. The black mamba relies on its speed to escape from snake eagles, which swoop down suddenly from trees and rocky outcrops and dodge the mamba's bites.

Even the most deadly snakes can themselves become prey.

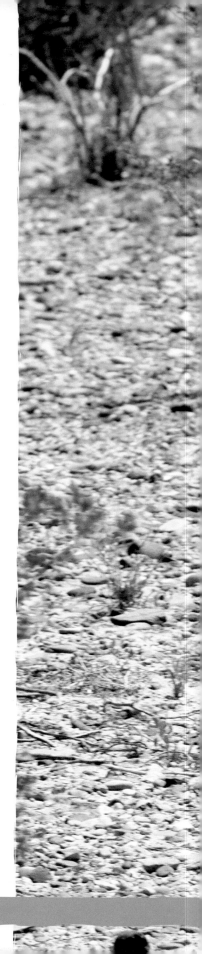

GETTING A HEAD START

A **prey** animal has a better chance of surviving if it can get away before the chasing **predator** reaches top speed. The prey may rely on such abilities as good hearing, sharp eyesight, or a keen sense of smell to sense approaching danger. A head start of even a fraction of a second can mean the difference between life and death.

The jack rabbit is a hare that lives in dry areas of western North America. Several predators, including coyotes, bobcats, and weasels, prey on jack rabbits. If chased, the jack rabbit can run as fast as 40 miles (65 kilometers) per hour, mixing its run with 10-foot (3-meter) leaps. Bobcats hunt jack rabbits by sneaking up on them and pouncing before they can reach top speed. A jack rabbit relies on its sharp hearing, eyesight, and sense of smell to sense danger and get a head start.

ZIGZAG ESCAPE

Some predators hunt best when traveling in a straight line at a steady speed. Prey animals can get away by changing their pace and direction. The cheetah, for example, is the fastest land animal, reaching speeds of 70 miles (110 kilometers) per hour as it chases down prey on the African **savanna.** None of its typical prey—such as gazelles, wildebeest calves, and smaller hoofed animals—can match its speed. Instead, the prey use special tactics to defend themselves. A high-speed chase uses much energy, so cheetahs need to catch their prey quickly—in less than a minute. To run away from a cheetah, an impala (a kind of antelope) often will run in a zigzag pattern. For the chasing cheetah, constantly changing direction and speed may burn up too much energy, forcing it to give up the chase.

Flyingfish

One of the most dramatic sights in tropical waters is the "flight" of flyingfish as they glide quickly through the air above the water. These small fish, usually about 8 to 12 inches (20 to 30 centimeters) long, do not really fly. Instead they build up speed in the water and then launch themselves into the air, steering with a pair of winglike fins as they glide up to 150 feet (45 meters). These leaps put flyingfish out of reach of larger predators such as sailfish, marlin, and tuna.

A flyingfish can stay in the air for more than 40 seconds as it leaps out of the water.

A jack rabbit runs and jumps between the creosote bushes in the south-western U.S. state of Texas.

You Can't Catch Me

It is possible for an animal to escape a **predator** without going anywhere, and without having to find somewhere to hide. That is how the springbok, a medium-sized African antelope, defends itself against speedy predators, such as cheetahs, hyenas, leopards, and wild dogs. It convinces predators to look somewhere else for their next meal.

The secret of the springbok's method is explained by its name, which comes from two Afrikaans words: *spring,* meaning jump, and *bok,* meaning antelope or goat. The name refers to the springbok's special habit of stotting—jumping straight up into the air from a standing start. Powerful back legs enable a springbok to leap more than 6 feet (1.8 meters) high, repeating the jump several times in a row.

Sometimes springboks stot as part of a mating display. The male springbok is sending a powerful message that it is strong and healthy. It is telling a potential **mate** that their offspring would also be strong and powerful.

More often, though, a springbok stots when it senses a predator approaching. The springbok is still signaling that it is strong and healthy, but this signal has a different meaning for a predator than for a potential mate. The impressive jumps let the predator know that the springbok has

The SPRINGBOK'S leap straight up into the air is called stotting.

spotted it and will start running away if it comes much closer. A predator would prefer to ambush its **prey,** or at least chase down a slower animal. With legs powerful enough to make such leaps, the stotting springbok shows that it would be extremely difficult to catch—especially with a head start. Rather than waste its energy on a chase that is likely to end in failure, the predator moves on to find slower prey. Both the springbok and the predator save energy by not taking part in a high-speed chase.

Body Work

People often use the word defense to refer to military weapons and fortresses. Animals can also fight back against their attackers, using their own bodies to repel (defeat), strike, or even trick **predators.**

TOO BIG TO FAIL

The blue whale is the largest animal that has ever lived, growing up to 100 feet (30 meters) long and weighing 150 tons (140 metric tons). The only creatures that try to attack blue whales are orcas (also called killer whales), which sometimes surround the larger whale and gang up on it. Such attacks are rare, though. A blue whale's huge size makes it immune to almost all attacks. In the same way, adult elephants have no natural predators because of their size. Lions will sometimes attack young or sick elephants if they stray from the herd, but a healthy, full-grown elephant is almost impossible for them to kill. Elephants only have to fear humans.

SMALL IS GOOD

Being tiny also has its defensive advantages. Small animals might not be worth the effort for a large predator. Hunting takes energy. If a predator hunts for an animal much smaller than it, the energy gained from eating the **prey** may be less than the energy spent to hunt. Grass rats—a type of mouse—can feed close to leopards and lions, which usually ignore them. Small animals are also harder to see and have an easier time finding places to hide. When a predator approaches, a small animal can quickly duck behind rocks or into a nook before it is even seen.

The huge size of
the blue whale makes it
almost impossible
to attack.

Puffing up

Pufferfish, common in tropical oceans, are clumsy
and slow swimmers. Their poor swimming abilities
should make them easy targets for the many
predators that live in tropical waters. But rather than
trying to swim away when threatened, a pufferfish
lives up to its name. The fish takes in huge amounts
of water or air into its stretchable stomach, swelling
up to three times normal size. If the sudden increase
in size is not enough to scare off predators, some
species of pufferfish also have **venomous** spines
that stick out when they puff up.

As the pufferfish
inflates, its long
spines stick out to
protect it.

LIVING FORTRESSES

Sometimes an animal's best defense is its own armor. A **prey** animal may prove too difficult to eat thanks to a stout shell, thick skin, or sharp spines.

Turtles are famous for defending themselves this way. When a **predator** approaches, most turtles can pull their heads—and often their limbs—into their hard shells. In some **species,** the front section of the lower shell is hinged. It slams shut against the upper shell when the turtle pulls its head inside, giving further protection. Most predators cannot break through this impressive defense.

Armadillos have poor eyesight, so they are not likely to spot their predators, such as jaguars, mountain lions, large snakes, and birds, in time to hide. But the name armadillo—*little armored one,* in Spanish—gives a clue to how these animals survive. Stiff plates cover the back, head, legs, and tail of an armadillo, offering excellent defense against attack. Some armadillo species curl up into a ball when attacked, so that their soft undersides are hidden. Others run away into thorny underbrush, using the same body armor to protect them from the thorns.

A three-banded armadillo rolls up into a ball for defense.

Seashells are familiar to anyone who has gone to the beach. The shells protect the **invertebrates** that live inside. Most of these shellfish are as soft as their land-based relatives, snails and slugs. The shells help protect them from predatory fish and seabirds.

Porcupine defense

Porcupines are **rodents** with an awesome defensive weapon—a coat of more than 30,000 needle-sharp quills that usually persuade a would-be predator to back off. The quills of some porcupine species can grow up to 1 foot (30 centimeters) long. They can drop off the porcupine and stick in an attacker's flesh, leaving a painful reminder to avoid porcupines in the future.

A porcupine shows its quills to an inquisitive lion cub.

The painted turtle relies on its hard shell for protection.

FIGHTING BACK

When other defenses fail, animals can use natural weapons to fight back. They can bite or kick a would-be **predator** or slash at it with horns. Though these defenses are a last resort, they can sometimes drive away attackers.

The gemsbok is a type of antelope found in dry areas of southern Africa. An adult has two sharp horns up to 4 feet (1.2 meters) long that sweep backward from its head. When attacked, it can put its head down, causing a predator to crash into the horns. Gemsboks have been known to kill attacking lions with this defense.

LOOK! A DISTRACTION!

Several animals use distracting behaviors to confuse predators. When caught, for example, the North American opossum "plays dead." It goes stiff, taking on the posture of a dead animal, and **secretes** a foul-smelling odor from scent **glands.** This apparent change of potential **prey** from an active animal to a dead one confuses predators. They often leave the opossum alone without eating it. The opossum is not acting— its behavior is a natural response to extreme stress, like fainting. Some snakes, such as the hognose, also play dead. The hognose coils up, rolls onto its back, opens its mouth wide, and sticks out its tongue. These behaviors make it look like it has died and dried out in the sun.

Other animals use different forms of distraction. **Cephalopods** squirt a cloud of black ink when threatened. This cloud hides them from a predator's view, giving them a chance to get away. Still others even drop off a part of their body to confuse attackers (see page 24).

Body Work

Leg power

Ostriches are large flightless birds of the African plains and deserts. Normally, the ostrich's speed and sharp eyesight help the bird to escape predators. Its long legs can take 15-foot (4.5-meter) steps at speeds up to 40 miles (65 kilometers) per hour. But if an ostrich is boxed in, it will kick with its strong legs. It also uses such kicks in defending its nest, which it cannot run away from. Ostriches can kill attackers with a powerful kick to the head.

A gemsbok has two long, sharp horns on its head.

An ostrich can't fly, but it can use its speed to escape from predators.

CUTTING LOSSES

Some animals can leave a part of their body behind if they are threatened. This action often confuses a chasing **predator,** giving the **prey** animal time to run away and survive.

Scientists use the word **autotomy** to describe this sort of defensive behavior. **Invertebrates** are more likely to use this method because it is easier for them to grow back lost body parts. Such animals as crickets, grasshoppers, and spiders can lose legs or **antennae** when attacked and grow them back. Crabs can drop a claw if they are alarmed.

Reptiles and **amphibians** are the **vertebrates** that most often use this trick. Geckos and other lizards will let their tails drop off if they are threatened. The discarded tail can twitch for several seconds, distracting a predator while the lizard gets away. Such lizards as geckos have special **tissues** inside their tails at the point where it separates from the body. Once the tail is lost, blood vessels leading to this point tighten and close, so the lizard loses very little blood. Some **species** can grow a new tail to replace the one they lost.

Letting loose

Sea cucumbers are not vegetables. They are distant relatives of sea stars and sea urchins. Sea cucumbers are covered with a soft, leathery skin, rather than hard spines like their relatives. When threatened, a sea cucumber can violently squeeze its muscles, shooting its internal **organs** out of its body. This action distracts a predator. Also, poison covers some of the **tissues** that connect the organs to the body. The sea cucumber grows these body parts back in several weeks.

A sea cucumber pushes out its insides in reaction to an attack.

This great earless lizard has lost its tail in self-defense.

Strength in Numbers

Animals often group together in large numbers. **Shoals** of fish, herds of cattle, colonies of **insects,** and flocks of birds are all examples. Joining in large groups offers many advantages. One of the most important is extra protection against **predators.**

GROUP BENEFITS

It might seem like large groups just make a bigger target for predators. In fact, animals lower their chances of being attacked when they join a group. In wide open settings, where there are few places to hide, being alone offers little protection against being spotted. If **prey** animals are all spread out, predators do not have to travel far to find them, and the lone prey might be less likely to spot approaching predators. With prey animals gathered in a group, predators may have to travel many miles or kilometers to find them. Herds also multiply the numbers of prey eyes and ears, any one set of which can tell the herd of a predator's approach.

Being in a group further benefits strong, healthy individuals. In the event of an attack, predators kill the first animals they can reach. In a herd, these are likely to be the slow, sick, old, or very young. As a result, the fast, healthy individuals are more likely to survive and reproduce.

Helping each other out

A herd is not all about self-preservation. Once in a while, group members may work together to help others. They might risk attack from predators to save a sick or wounded individual. For example, African buffalo have been known to risk their lives to rescue herd members from predators.

Fish called mackerel swim together in a group for protection against predators.

Female and young buffalo are usually placed at the center of buffalo herds for greater safety.

ON THE LOOKOUT

One of the most basic advantages of a herd is having extra pairs of eyes, ears, and nostrils to sense danger. The East African plains are full of green grass after each rainy season. At this time, huge herds of grazing animals—often of different **species**—gather to eat together. Individual animals on the edge of the herd act as lookouts. Using sharp eyesight and hearing, they scan for signs of **predators** while the other herd members graze. If an individual spots approaching danger, it will signal the rest of the herd with calls or body movements, telling them to beware or possibly run away.

CONFUSING PREDATORS

Animals can use stripes, spots, or other patterns on their bodies to confuse predators. The patterns from one animal blend into those of its neighbors. This tactic is called disruptive coloration. Disruptive coloration makes it hard for predators to make out individual animals in the group. Zebras' stripes are an excellent example of disruptive coloration. They make it difficult for a lion or hyena to single out a particular zebra to attack.

Even without disruptive coloration, a swirling mass of **prey** can confuse a predator, making it harder to target an individual animal. A huge **shoal** of mackerel looks like a single, silvery body as it speeds through the water. Gathering in this way makes it difficult for predatory fish to target a meal.

Animals instinctively swirl and push toward the center of a herd. An *instinct* is something an animal is born knowing how to do. Sheep show such behavior in response to herding by a sheepdog. Although sheep have been tame for thousands of years, they instinctively react to the dog as if it were a predator and gather themselves into a tight, swirling herd.

Meerkat sentries

Small **mammals** called meerkats live in dry, open areas of southern Africa. Close-knit groups of about 50 meerkats share an underground burrow dug in the sandy soil. Away from the protection of the burrow, meerkats may be attacked by predatory birds and snakes. Each group has a "sentry" who keeps watch for approaching danger. The sentry barks if it senses trouble, sending the mob scurrying to the safety of the burrow.

A meerkat sentry keeps watch on the burrow.

Zebra stripes make it difficult to pick out individual animals.

GROUP ATTACK

Once in a while, a group of animals will gang up to attack potential **predators.** This behavior is called **mobbing.** Flocks of birds are known for this behavior. Crows will mob larger birds that try to rob their nests. They will dive at the larger bird, sometimes veering away, sometimes crashing into and pecking it in midair. Other crows, noticing the conflict, join in on the attack. As many as 100 birds may join in driving the hunter away.

HIVE DEFENSE

The Asian giant hornet can quickly destroy beehives. A scout hornet finds a beehive and flies away to tell other giant hornets. The group of hornets breaks into the hive and kills the smaller honey bees. Bees cannot sting through the hornets' thick armor, so they are helpless against such an attack.

Some kinds of Asian honey bees have developed a special defense to prevent a hornet invasion. When a giant hornet scout enters the hive, all the bees fly to it. The hornet may kill the first few defenders, but the bees quickly cover the invader, preventing it from flying away. Once the bees have trapped the scout, they begin to shiver their wings and bodies, making heat. After a while, the trapped hornet overheats and dies. Some of the honey bees also overheat and die. Though many honey bees die while stopping the scout, this method prevents the total destruction of the hive.

The Asian giant hornet is protected by thick body armor.

A white-tailed eagle is mobbed by crows.

Whale mobbing

In a remarkable case of mobbing, pods (small groups) of humpback whales will come together to try to stop the hunting and feeding of orcas. Humpbacks sometimes rescue other humpbacks that have been singled out by the orcas, but they also rescue other **species** of whales, dolphins, seals, and even ocean sunfish. One or more humpbacks will shield the **prey** animal with their bodies while others slash at the orcas with their huge fins and tails.

Noble Sacrifice

The natural world has other examples of animals that sacrifice their lives to protect the group. One of the most dramatic examples comes from a **species** of termite in the South American tropics. Known only by its scientific name, *Neocapritermes taracua* (*nee yoh kap rih TEHR mees tah rah KYU uh*), this termite lives in the rain forests of French Guiana, a French territory on the northern coast of South America. Like bees and other **eusocial insects,** the termites live together in nests, with individuals carrying out specific jobs.

Worker termites find food and keep up the nest. **Glands** in their **abdomens secrete** blue crystals, which form a poisonous liquid when mixed with saliva. The liquid is stored in a pouch on the termite's back. When the workers are too old to perform their usual tasks—usually because their **mandibles** have become blunt—they can still help the nest by sacrificing themselves.

If the nest is attacked, the older workers join soldier termites in the battle. The workers rush into the fray and cause their poison pouches to explode. This attack usually kills the invaders as well as the workers.

This special form of self-sacrifice in defense of a group is called autothysis (*aw TAHTH uh sihs*). Individuals of other termite species and some ants also use their own deaths to protect others. Some of them make a sticky substance, which—along with the dead insect's body—can block tunnels so invaders cannot get in.

WORKER HONEY BEES may sacrifice themselves to protect the hive.

In many species of bees, individuals give up their lives for the good of the hive. Worker honey bees can only sting once. When a worker stings, its barbed stinger sticks in its target and pulls out of the bee's body. The worker bee dies soon after losing its stinger, but the sting has helped to protect the hive.

Acting Up

Simply blending in with the background—the secret of **camouflage** (see pages 6-11)—is not enough for some animals. They can use **mimicry** to look or act like bad-tasting or dangerous creatures. A **predator** knows better than to attack something that could injure it or make it ill.

PLAYING TOUGH

One way an animal can scare off predators is to make itself look more dangerous than it is. The frilled lizard lives in Australia and the southern part of the nearby large island of New Guinea. It can grow up to 3 feet (0.9 meter) long, but it is scrawny, and more than half of its length is tail. But the lizard can unleash a secret weapon to startle predators. It can extend a large frill, up to 1 foot (0.3 meter) across, behind its head. If the predator is not scared away by the sudden opening of the frill, it may still think twice before attacking an animal that looks much larger than it did a second ago.

Some moths have markings called eyespots on the tops of their wings. When a moth lands on an upright surface, such as the trunk of a tree, its open wings may look like the face of an owl or other predatory bird. Predators may pause before attacking such a frightening creature.

A South American frog that lives on the Brazilian **savanna** takes the fake-eye disguise a step further. It has markings that look like eyes just above its back legs. The frog inflates its body when threatened by a predator—either a bird or a giant water bug. The eyespots get bigger as the frog's body inflates, so that the predator seems to be faced with a larger opponent.

Its neck frill makes this lizard look much bigger than it really is.

Snake or caterpillar?

Some **species** of caterpillar have eyespots on their tails to help delay or prevent attacks. Seen from above—by a hungry bird, for example—the eyespots look like real eyes, and the caterpillar may look like a small snake staring back. Attackers may be fooled by this disguise, preferring to avoid a fight with a dangerous snake.

The tail end of an oleander hawk moth caterpillar has eye markings to fool predators.

LOOKING DEADLY

Many animals defend themselves through disguise as deadlier creatures. Several **species** of fly have black and yellow stripes to look like stinging bees, wasps, and hornets. After seeing this color pattern, most **predators** will not give the fly a second look.

The fear of dangerous animals may run so deep that it continues to protect a **mimic** long after the more dangerous animal has disappeared. The grassy pine forests of the Carolina Sandhills, in the southeastern United States, were once the home to the highly **venomous** coral snake. The nonvenomous kingsnake that lives there protects itself with markings that look like the coral snake's red, yellow, and black patterns. No coral snakes have been reported in the sandhills for nearly 60 years, but raccoons, birds, and bears still instinctively avoid the kingsnake.

Scientists think that matching a dangerous animal's particular colors is the first step in becoming a successful mimic. Most animals pick up on color more readily than patterns. Over many generations, the mimics "fine tune" their look to take on the blotches, stripes, and other patterns of their deadly disguise.

DIVERTING ATTENTION

Many ground-nesting birds use a type of **mimicry** not to defend themselves, but to protect their young. As a predator approaches the nest, the parent bird drags one wing on the ground and hops away, squawking loudly. This act catches the attention of the predator, which may think the adult bird has a broken wing and will be easy to catch. After the adult has led the predator away from the nest, it gives up the act and flies away.

A killdeer pretends to have a broken wing to draw attention away from its nest.

Rodent run

The bird called the purple sandpiper, which lives in the Arctic tundra, performs an elaborate diversion act. It mimics a small **mammal** running away from its nest—an easy meal for a predator. The sandpiper drags both its wings to look like it has a second pair of legs, fluffs up its feathers to look more like fur, and "squeals" as it zigzags across the ground in a **rodent**-like run.

This brightly striped kingsnake mimics the coloring of the venomous coral snake.

A CLOSER LOOK

Octopus Escape Artists

Octopuses are remarkable animals, combining intelligence, flexibility, and changing color patterns to hide from—or escape—**predators.** Scientists have even filmed a 600-pound (270-kilogram) giant octopus squeezing through a gap no wider than an inch (2.5 centimeters). And if these skills are not enough, octopuses can **secrete** a dense cloud of ink to mask their escape (see page 22).

One of the most dramatic octopus defenses is changing skin color and even texture at a moment's notice (see page 8). This ability enables octopuses to **camouflage** themselves against almost any background. They can blend in so well that even sharp-eyed predators cannot see them.

Some octopuses can **mimic** the behavior of other sea creatures. One **species,** called the mimic octopus, stands out from the rest. It lives in tropical waters around the southeast Asian country of Indonesia. The mimic octopus can change its color and shape to look like as many as 16 other creatures. One moment, it can look like a sea snake. Then, it can change into a brightly colored lionfish, before turning into a flatfish disguised against the sandy sea floor. It does not just mimic its subject's

The MIMIC OCTOPUS changes itself to look like a flatfish against the sea floor.

shape and color. It also copies the swimming and movement patterns of these animals. Potential predators avoid the octopus, mistaking it for any number of poisonous or foul-tasting creatures.

There's even another animal that uses the mimic octopus to hide itself. When escaping from a predator, the tiny black-marble jawfish can change color to blend into an octopus's impression of a hermit crab, lionfish, or other sea creature.

Spraying, Shocking, and Stinging

Sometimes, an animal is easy to spot and catch and too weak to fight back. These animals may have unusual defenses against attack.

POWERFUL SMELLS

The odor of a skunk is unmistakeable. It is bad enough to sniff one from a distance. If you happen to get sprayed, you are doomed to smell terrible for days. How do you get rid of the smell—hose down, take a bath in tomato juice, or just get rid of your old clothes and hope it goes away? A potential animal attacker is put off by such an awful smell just as much as a human is.

The secret to the skunk's stink is in **glands** at its rear. These glands make a liquid called **musk.** Muscles near the glands give the skunk excellent aim, so that the spray can hit a target up to 15 feet (4.5 meters) away. The skunk aims for an enemy's eyes, because the musk can cause temporary blindness. The glands only hold enough musk for about five sprays—and it can take up to two weeks to make more—so the skunk is careful about using this powerful defense.

Skunks are not the only animal **species** to call on foul smells for defense. Sea hares (a type of sea slug), opossums (see page 22), and millipedes are among the most notable stinkers. Birds can also use the "stink defense." Vultures are **scavengers,** animals that eat the dead bodies of other animals. If threatened, a vulture may defend itself by simply vomiting. The awful stench of stomach acids combined with rotting flesh is enough to drive most **predators** away.

Gumming up the works

The hagfish, a deep-sea scavenger looking like a small eel, has a special way of putting off predators. When attacked, it quickly **secretes** gobs of slimy **mucus.** The mucus fills the attacker's mouth and gill slits. Unable to breathe properly, the shark or fish spits out the hagfish as it tries to clear out the sticky mucus.

The hagfish can suffocate an attacker with sticky, slimy mucus.

A skunk raises its tail in preparation for a musk attack.

DANGEROUS SPRAYS

Aside from the skunk, other animals can squirt unpleasant liquids at their **prey.** If the bombardier beetle is disturbed, it may release a hot, posionous liquid that can injure and even kill attacking **insects.** The liquid is a mixture of two chemicals stored in separate "tanks" in the beetle's **abdomen.** When the beetle is disturbed, the chemicals mix together and react. Heat from the reaction raises the mixture to a scorching 200 °F (95 °C). The reaction releases a gas that propels the liquid out with a loud "pop."

The bombardier beetle sprays attackers with a stream of hot chemicals.

The Texas horned lizard could make an easy snack for a coyote or bobcat prowling through the desert landscape. The lizard's coloring helps it blend into its surroundings, but keen-eyed **predators** still sometimes spot it. When cornered or attacked, the lizard turns and squirts nasty-tasting blood from its eyes, straight into the attacker's mouth. A predator is usually so startled by this response that it lets go of the lizard and runs away.

POISON WEAPONS

Just as people must avoid some kinds of foods, some predators stay away from animals that can sicken or kill them. The cane toad has poison **glands** and is deadly to most animals that try to eat it. The giant toads were brought to Australia in an attempt to control pest insects, but they ate all the food of many native Australian animals, driving them toward **extinction.** Eating the poisonous toad has killed millions of native predators that do not instinctively know to leave them alone.

Some animals eat particular poisonous living things for defense. Instead of being sickened or killed, they can store the poison in their bodies. The **larva**—caterpillar—of the monarch butterfly feeds on the poisonous milkweed plant, making the insect dangerous and bad-tasting to predators. The poison dart frog accumulates deadly toxins by eating poisonous insects.

Electric attacks

Humans began using electricity in the late 1800's. But some animals have been tapping into its power for millions of years. The electric eel has special **organs** that can create electric charges of up to 650 volts—more than 300 times the power of a flashlight battery. The eel uses this electric charge to zap and stun jaguars, snakes, crocodiles, and other powerful predators in its South American **habitat.**

An electric eel can grow up to 8 feet (2.5 meters) long.

The Texas horned lizard can squirt foul-tasting blood at its attackers.

VENOMOUS DEFENSE

Venom is poison that is injected into a victim by an animal's fangs, barbs, or other sharp growths or **organs.** Venom is often used by **predators** to attack **prey,** but a predator will not hesitate to use its venom when it is attacked. Spitting cobras spray their powerful venom into the eyes of attackers. The Sydney funnel-web spider has a venom powerful enough to kill a human in 15 minutes. Usually, the spider uses its venom to quickly kill the **invertebrates** it eats. It only bites humans when startled or threatened.

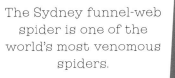
The Sydney funnel-web spider is one of the world's most venomous spiders.

A few animals make venom only for defense. Stingrays, flat fish related to sharks, have **venomous** stingers in their tails. They only use this weapon in self-defense, usually when startled. The stonefish, a coral reef native, is the most venomous fish in the world. It has 13 spines on its back, connected to pouches full of venom. Surprisingly, the stonefish does not use these spines to hunt for food. It relies on its excellent **camouflage** and sudden bursts of speed to catch prey. Instead, the venom is used against predators, such as sea snakes. Unlucky swimmers and divers who step on stonefish need immediate treatment to prevent **paralysis** and even death.

Venomous animals must sucessfully bite or sting for their venom to be of any use in repelling predators. Venom must enter an animal's blood or body fluid to work. Unlike poisonous animals (see page 42), a predator is not harmed just by eating venomous prey.

Venomous mammal

Most venomous animals are **insects,** fish, and **reptiles.** But a few **mammals** can make venom, too. The duck-billed platypus is a strange aquatic mammal that lives on the continent of Australia. Male platypuses have a hollow, clawlike spur on each ankle connected to venom **glands.** Males usually use these spurs while fighting with other males for **mates.** But they will also use the venomous spines in defense if threatened. This chemical is powerful enough to **paralyze** an attacker—and even cause extreme pain to an unlucky human.

A stonefish can be very difficult to spot on the sea floor.

Glossary

abdomen the rear part of an arthropod's body. An arthropod is an animal with jointed legs and no backbone.

algae a simple living thing that can make its own food.

amphibian a vertebrate with scaleless skin that usually lives part of its life in water and part on land.

antenna (plural antennae) a long, delicate sense organ, or feeler, found on the heads of various invertebrates, including insects.

autotomy the deliberate casting off of a body part by a threatened animal.

camouflage the natural coloring or form of an animal that enables it to blend into its surroundings, making it difficult to see.

cephalopod a group of predatory mollusks that includes octopuses and squid. Mollusks are a group of soft-bodied invertebrates.

chromatophore a cell in an animal's skin that contains pigments, enabling the animal to alter its coloring.

eusocial describes an animal that lives in a large, highly organized colony where only certain members reproduce and others animals cooperate to raise young and maintain the colony.

extinction when every member of a species (kind) of living thing has died.

gland an organ in an animal's body that secretes (gives off) chemical substances for use in the body or for release into the surroundings.

habitat the place where a living thing usually makes its home.

insect one of the major invertebrate groups. Insects have six legs and a three-part body.

invertebrate an animal without a backbone.

larva (plural larvae) the active, immature stage of some animals, such as many insects, that is different from its adult form.

mammal one of the major vertebrate animal groups. Mammals feed their offspring on milk produced by the mother, and most have hair or fur.

mandible either half of the crushing organ in an arthropod's mouthparts. An arthropod is an animal with jointed legs and no backbone.

mate the animal with which another animal partners to reproduce (to make more animals like the two that are mating); the act of mating, when two animals come together to reproduce.

mimic to copy something, or the close external resemblance of an animal to something else; an animal that does this.

mimicry the action of copying something, or the close external resemblance of an animal to something else.

mobbing a behavior in which a group of smaller animals, such as birds, attack a predator to drive it away.

mucus a thick liquid that is produced in parts of animals' bodies.

musk a distinct scent given off by certain animals.

nocturnality the condition of being active at night, or nocturnal.

organ a part of the body, made of similar cells and cell tissue, that performs a particular function.

paralysis the loss of the ability to move.

paralyze to make a living thing unable to move.

pigment the natural coloring matter of animal tissue.

Find Out More

predator an animal that hunts, kills, and eats other animals.

prey an animal that is hunted, killed, and eaten by another.

reptile one of the major vertebrate animal groups. A reptile has dry, scaly skin and breathes air. Snakes, crocodiles, and lizards are all reptiles.

rodent a mammal with front teeth made for gnawing hard things.

roost a place where a group of animals, particularly birds, regularly sleeps; the act of roosting.

savanna grasslands with widely scattered bushes and trees.

scavenger an animal that feeds on the carcasses of dead animals.

shoal a group of fish.

secrete to produce a liquid naturally.

species a group of living things that have certain permanent traits in common and are able to reproduce with each other.

tissue the material of which living things are made.

venom a naturally produced liquid that animals can introduce into other animals (for example, through biting) in order to stun, injure, or kill the other animal.

venomous describes an animal that produces venom or a part of such an animal that releases venom.

vertebrate an animal with a backbone.

zooplankton tiny living things that drift at or near the surface of oceans, lakes, and other bodies of water.

BOOKS

Animal Defenses by Mary Lindeen (Chicago: Norwood House Press, 2017)

Exploding Ants and Other Amazing Defenses by Rebecca E. Hirsch (Minneapolis: Lerner Publications, 2017)

Invisible to the Eye: Animals in Disguise by Kendra Muntz (Chicago: World Book, 2014)

Life in the Wild by Michael Chinery (London: Armadillo Pub., 2013)

Why Do Animals Hide? by Robin Koontz (Vero Beach, FL: Rourke Educational Media, 2016)

WEBSITES

National Wildlife Federation's Blog
http://blog.nwf.org/2016/02/defensive-mimicry-wild-wizards-of-trickery-and-illusions/
Describes several animals that use mimicry to avoid predators.

National Wildlife Refuge Association
http://www.refugeassociation.org/
An organization promoting the creation and protection of wildlife refuges within the United States.

Serengeti National Park
http://www.serengeti.org/
The official website of Serengeti National Park in Tanzania.

Index